DEIRDRE OF THE SORROWS

By J. M. SYNGE

JOHN W. LUCE & COMPANY
BOSTON : : : : : : : 1911

DEIRDRE OF THE SORROWS

PERSONS IN THE PLAY

LAVARCHAM, *Deirdre's nurse*

OLD WOMAN, *Lavarcham's servant*

OWEN, *Conchubor's attendant and spy*

CONCHUBOR, *High King of Ulster*

FERGUS, *Conchubor's friend*

DEIRDRE

NAISI, *Deirdre's lover*

AINNLE, *Naisi's brother*

ARDAN, *Naisi's brother*

TWO SOLDIERS

ACT I.

*Lavarcham's house
on Slieve Fuadh.*

DEIRDRE OF THE SORROWS

ACT I

Lavarcham's house on Slieve Fuadh. There is a door to inner room on the left, and a door to open air on the right. Window at back and a frame with a half-finished piece of tapestry. There are also a large press and heavy oak chest near the back wall. The place is neat and clear but bare. Lavarcham, woman of fifty, is working at tapestry frame. Old Woman comes in from left.

OLD WOMAN. She hasn't come yet, is it, and it falling to the night?

LAVARCHAM. She has not. . . (*Concealing her anxiety.*) It's dark with the clouds are coming from the west and south, but it isn't later than the common.

OLD WOMAN. It's later, surely, and I hear tell the Sons of Usna, Naisi and his brothers, are above chasing hares for two days or three, and the same awhile since when the moon was full.

LAVARCHAM — *more anxiously.*— The gods send they don't set eyes on her — (*with a sign of helplessness*) yet if they do itself, it wasn't my wish brought them or could send them away.

OLD WOMAN—*r e p r o v i n g l y.*—If it wasn't, you'd do well to keep a check on her, and she turning a woman that was meant to be a queen.

LAVARCHAM. Who'd check her like was meant to have her pleasure only, the way if there were no warnings told about her you'd see troubles coming when an old king is taking her, and she without a thought but for her beauty and to be straying the hills.

OLD WOMAN. The gods help the lot of us. . . . Shouldn't she be well pleased getting the like of Conchubor, and he middling settled in his years itself? I don't know what he wanted putting her this wild place to be breaking her in, or putting myself to be roasting her supper and she with no patience for her food at all.   [*She looks out.*

LAVARCHAM. Is she coming from the glen?

OLD WOMAN. She is not. But whisht — there's two men leaving the furze — (*crying out*) its Conchubor and Fergus along with him. Conchubor'll be in a blue stew this night and herself abroad.

LAVARCHAM — *settling room hastily.*— Are they close by?

OLD WOMAN. Crossing the stream, and there's herself on the hillside with a load of twigs. Will I run out and put her in order before they'll set eyes on her at all?

LAVARCHAM. You will not. Would you have him see you, and he a man would be jealous of a hawk would fly between her and the rising sun. (*She looks out.*) Go up to the hearth and be as busy as if you hadn't seen them at all.

OLD WOMAN — *sitting down to polish vessel.*— There'll be trouble this night, for he should be in his tempers from the way he's stepping out, and he swinging his hands.

LAVARCHAM — *wearied with the whole matter.*— It'd be best of all, maybe, if he got in tempers with herself, and made an end quickly, for I'm in a poor way between the pair of them (*going back to tapestry frame.*) There they are now at the door.

[*Conchubor and Fergus come in.*

CONCHUBOR AND FERGUS. The gods save you.

LAVARCHAM — *getting up and courtesying.*— The gods save and keep you kindly, and stand between you and all harm for ever.

CONCHUBOR—*looking around.*—Where is Deirdre?

LAVARCHAM — *trying to speak with indifference.*— Abroad upon Slieve Fuadh. She does be all times straying around picking flowers or nuts, or sticks itself; but so long as she's gathering new life I've a right not to heed her, I'm thinking, and she taking her will.

[*Fergus talks to Old Woman.*

CONCHUBOR — *stiffly.*— A night with thunder coming is no night to be abroad.

LAVARCHAM — *more uneasily.*— She's used to every track and pathway, and the lightning itself wouldn't let down its flame to singe the beauty of her like.

FERGUS — *cheerfully.*— She's right, Conchubor, and let you sit down and take your ease, (*he takes a wallet from under his cloak*) and I'll count out what we've brought, and put it in the presses within.

[*He goes into the inner room with the Old Woman.*

CONCHUBOR — *sitting down and looking about.*— Where are the mats and hangings and the silver skillets I sent up for Deirdre?

LAVARCHAM. The mats and hangings are in this press, Conchubor. She wouldn't wish to be soiling them, she said, running out

and in with mud and grasses on her feet, and
it raining since the night of Samhain. The
silver skillets and the golden cups we have
beyond locked in the chest.

CONCHUBOR. Bring them out and use
them from this day.

LAVARCHAM. We'll do it, Conchubor.

CONCHUBOR — *getting up and going to
frame.*— Is this hers?

LAVARCHAM — *pleased to speak of it.*—
It is, Conchubor. All say there isn't her match
at fancying figures and throwing purple upon
crimson, and she edging them all times with
her greens and gold.

CONCHUBOR — *a little uneasily.*— Is she
keeping wise and busy since I passed before,
and growing ready for her life in Emain?

LAVARCHAM — *dryly.*— That is a ques-
tion will give small pleasure to yourself or me.
(*Making up her mind to speak out.*) If it's
the truth I'll tell you, she's growing too wise
to marry a big king and she a score only. Let
you not be taking it bad, Conchubor, but you'll
get little good seeing her this night, for with
all my talking it's wilfuller she's growing these
two months or three.

CONCHUBOR — *severely, but relieved
things are no worse.*— Isn't it a poor thing

you're doing so little to school her to meet what is to come?

LAVARCHAM. I'm after serving you two score of years, and I'll tell you this night, Conchubor, she's little call to mind an old woman when she has the birds to school her, and the pools in the rivers where she goes bathing in the sun. I'll tell you if you seen her that time, with her white skin, and her red lips, and the blue water and the ferns about her, you'd know, maybe, and you greedy itself, it wasn't for your like she was born at all.

CONCHUBOR. It's little I heed for what she was born; she'll be my comrade, surely.

[*He examines her workbox.*

LAVARCHAM — *sinking into sadness again.*— I'm in dread so they were right saying she'd bring destruction on the world, for it's a poor thing when you see a settled man putting the love he has for a young child, and the love he has for a full woman, on a girl the like of her; and it's a poor thing, Conchubor, to see a High King, the way you are this day, prying after her needles and numbering her lines of thread.

CONCHUBOR — *getting .up.*— Let you not be talking too far and you old itself.

(*Walks across room and back.*) Does she know the troubles are foretold?

LAVARCHAM — *in the tone of the earlier talk.*— I'm after telling her one time and another, but I'd do as well speaking to a lamb of ten weeks and it racing the hills. . . . It's not the dread of death or troubles that would tame her like.

CONCHUBOR — *he looks out.*— She's coming now, and let you walk in and keep Fergus till I speak with her a while.

LAVARCHAM — *going left.*— If I'm after vexing you itself, it'd be best you weren't taking her hasty or scolding her at all.

CONCHUBOR — *very stiffly.*— I've no call to. I'm well pleased she's light and airy.

LAVARCHAM — *offended at his tone.*— Well pleased is it? (*With a snort of irony*) It's a queer thing the way the likes of me do be telling the truth, and the wise are lying all times.

> [*She goes into room on left. Conchubor arranges himself before a mirror for a moment, then goes a little to the left and waits. Deirdre comes in poorly dressed, with a little bag and a bundle of twigs in her arms. She is astonished for a moment when she sees Conchu-*

bor; then she makes a courtesy to him, and goes to the hearth without any embarrassment.

CONCHUBOR. The gods save you, Deirdre. I have come up bringing you rings and jewels from Emain Macha.

DEIRDRE. The gods save you.

CONCHUBOR. What have you brought from the hills?

DEIRDRE — *quite self-possessed.* — A bag of nuts, and twigs for our fires at the dawn of day.

CONCHUBOR — *showing annoyance in spite of himself.* — And it's that way you're picking up the manners will fit you to be Queen of Ulster?

DEIRDRE — *made a little defiant by his tone.* — I have no wish to be a queen.

CONCHUBOR — *a l m o s t sneeringly.* — You'd wish to be dressing in your duns and grey, and you herding your geese or driving your calves to their shed — like the common lot scattered in the glens.

DEIRDRE — *very defiant.* — I would not, Conchubor. (*She goes to tapestry and begins to work.*) A girl born the way I'm born is more likely to wish for a mate who'd be her likeness. . . . A man with his hair like the raven, maybe, and his skin like the snow and his lips like blood spilt on it.

CONCHUBOR — *sees his mistake, and after a moment takes a flattering tone, looking at her work.*— Whatever you wish, there's no queen but would be well pleased to have your skill at choosing colours and making pictures on the cloth. (*Looking closely.*) What is it you're figuring?

DEIRDRE — *deliberately.*— Three young men and they chasing in the green gap of a wood.

CONCHUBOR — *now almost pleading.*— It's soon you'll have dogs with silver chains to be chasing in the woods of Emain, for I have white hounds rearing up for you, and grey horses, that I've chosen from the finest in Ulster and Britain and Gaul.

DEIRDRE — *unmoved as before.*— I've heard tell, in Ulster and Britain and Gaul, Naisi and his brothers have no match and they chasing in the woods.

CONCHUBOR — *very gravely.*— Isn't it a strange thing you'd be talking of Naisi and his brothers, or figuring them either, when you know the things that are foretold about themselves and you? Yet you've little knowledge, and I'd do wrong taking it bad when it'll be

my share from this out to keep you the way
you'll have little call to trouble for knowledge,
or its want either.

DEIRDRE.   Yourself should be wise,
surely.

CONCHUBOR.   The like of me has a
store of knowledge that's a weight and terror.
It's for that we do choose out the like of yourself that are young and glad only. . . . I'm
thinking you are gay and lively each day in
the year?

DEIRDRE.   I don't know if that's true,
Conchubor.   There are lonesome days and bad
nights in this place like another.

CONCHUBOR.   You should have as few
sad days, I'm thinking, as I have glad and
good ones.

DEIRDRE.   What is it has you that way
ever coming this place, when you'd hear the
old woman saying a good child's as happy as
a king?

CONCHUBOR.   How would I be happy
seeing age coming on me each year, when the
dry leaves are blowing back and forward at
the gate of Emain?   And yet this last while
I'm saying out, when I see the furze breaking
and the daws sitting two and two on ash-trees
by the duns of Emain, Deirdre's a year nearer

her full age when she'll be my mate and comrade, and then I'm glad surely.

DEIRDRE — *almost to herself.*— I will not be your mate in Emain.

CONCHUBOR — *not heeding her.*— It's there you'll be proud and happy and you'll learn that, if young men are great hunters, yet it's with the like of myself you'll find a knowledge of what is priceless in your own like. What we all need is a place is safe and splendid, and it's that you'll get in Emain in two days or three.

DEIRDRE — *aghast.*— Two days!

CONCHUBOR. I have the rooms ready, and in a little while you'll be brought down there, to be my queen and queen of the five parts of Ireland.

DEIRDRE — *standing up frightened and pleading.*— I'd liefer stay this place, Conchubor. . . . Leave me this place, where I'm well used to the tracks and pathways and the people of the glens. . . . It's for this life I'm born, surely.

CONCHUBOR. You'll be happier and greater with myself in Emain. It is I will be your comrade, and will stand between you and the great troubles are foretold.

DEIRDRE. I will not be your queen in

Emain when it's my pleasure to be having my freedom on the edges of the hills.

CONCHUBOR. It's my wish to have you quickly; I'm sick and weary thinking of the day you'll be brought down to me, and seeing you walking into my big, empty halls. I've made all sure to have you, and yet all said there's a fear in the back of my mind I'd miss you and have great troubles in the end. It's for that, Deirdre, I'm praying that you'll come quickly; and you may take the word of a man has no lies, you'll not find, with any other, the like of what I'm bringing you in wildness and confusion in my own mind.

DEIRDRE. I cannot go, Conchubor.

CONCHUBOR — *taking a triumphant tone.*— It is my pleasure to have you, and I a man is waiting a long while on the throne of Ulster. Wouldn't you liefer be my comrade, growing up the like of Emer and Maeve, than to be in this place and you a child always?

DEIRDRE. You don't know me and you'd have little joy taking me, Conchubor. . . . I'm a long while watching the days getting a great speed passing me by. I'm too long taking my will, and it's that way I'll be living always.

CONCHUBOR — *dryly.*— Call Fergus to

come with me.   This is your last night upon
Slieve Puadh.

DEIRDRE — *now pleadingly.*— Leave me
a short space longer, Conchubor.   Isn't it a
poor thing I should be hastened away, when
all these troubles are foretold?   Leave me a
year, Conchubor; it isn't much I'm asking.

CONCHUBOR.   It's much to have me
two score and two weeks waiting for your
voice in Emain, and you in this place growing
lonesome and shy.   I'm a ripe man and in
great love, and yet, Deirdre, I'm the King of
Ulster.   (*He gets up.*)   I'll call Fergus, and
we'll make Emain ready in the morning.

[*He goes towards door on left.*

DEIRDRE — *clinging to him.*— Do not
call him, Conchubor. . . .   Promise me a year
of quiet. . . .   It's one year I'm asking only.

CONCHUBOR.   You'd be asking a year
next year, and the years that follow.   (*Calling.*)   Fergus! Fergus!   (*To Deirdre.*)
Young girls are slow always; it is their lovers
that must say the word.   (*Calling.*)   Fergus!

[*Deirdre springs away from him as
Fergus comes in with Lavarcham and
the Old Woman.*

CONCHUBOR — *to Fergus.*— There is a

storm coming, and we'd best be going to our people when the night is young.)

FERGUS — *cheerfully*.— The gods shield you, Deirdre. (*To Conchubor*.) We're late already, and it's no work the High King to be slipping on stepping-stones and hilly pathways when the floods are rising with the rain.

[*He helps Conchubor into his cloak.*

CONCHUBOR — *glad that he has made his decision — to Lavarcham.*— Keep your rules a few days longer, and you'll be brought down to Emain, you and Deirdre with you.)

LAVARCHAM—*obediently.*— Your rules are kept always.

CONCHUBOR.   The gods shield you.

[*He goes out with Fergus.   Old Woman bolts door.*

LAVARCHAM — *looking at Dierdre, who has covered her face.*— Wasn't I saying you'd do it? You've brought your marriage a sight nearer not heeding those are wiser than yourself.

DEIRDRE — *with agitation.*— It wasn't I did it.   Will you take me from this place, Lavarcham, and keep me safe in the hills?

LAVARCHAM.   He'd have us tracked in the half of a day, and then you'd be his queen

in spite of you, and I and mine would be
destroyed for ever.

DEIRDRE — *terrified with the reality that
is before her.*— Are there none can go against
Conchubor?

LAVARCHAM. Maeve of Connaught
only, and those that are her like.

DEIRDRE. Would Fergus go against
him?

LAVARCHAM. He would, maybe, and
his temper roused.

DEIRDRE — *in a lower voice with sudden
excitement.*— Would Naisi and his brothers?

LAVARCHAM — *impatiently.*— Let you
not be dwelling on Naisi and his brothers. . . .
In the end of all there is none can go against
Conchubor, and it's folly that we're talking,
for if any went against Conchubor it's sorrow
he'd earn and the shortening of his day of life.

[*She turns away, and Deirdre stands up
stiff with excitement and goes and
looks out of the window.*

DEIRDRE. Are the stepping-stones flooding, Lavarcham? Will the night be stormy in
the hills?

LAVARCHAM — *looking at her curiously.*
The stepping-stones are flooding, surely, and

the night will be the worst, I'm thinking, we've seen these years gone by.

DEIRDRE — *tearing open the press and pulling out clothes and tapestries.*— Lay these mats and hangings by the windows, and at the tables for our feet, and take out the skillets of silver, and the golden cups we have, and our two flasks of wine.

LAVARCHAM.   What ails you?

DEIRDRE — *gathering up a dress.*— Lay them out quickly, Lavarcham, we've no call dawdling this night. Lay them out quickly; I'm going into the room to put on the rich dresses and jewels have been sent from Emain.

LAVARCHAM.   Putting on dresses at this hour, and it dark and drenching with the weight of rain!   Are you away in your head?

DEIRDRE — *gathering her things together with an outburst of excitement.*— I will dress like Emer in Dundealgan, or Meave in her house in Connaught. ✓ If Conchubor'll make me a queen, I'll have the right of a queen who is a master, taking her own choice and making a stir to the edges of the seas. . . . Lay out your mats and hangings where I can stand this night and look about me. Lay out the skins of the rams of Connaught and of the goats of the west. I will not be a child or plaything; I'll put on my robes that are the richest, for I will not be brought down to Emain as Cuchulain brings his horse to the yoke, or Conall Cearneach puts his shield upon his arm; and maybe from this day I will turn the men of Ireland like a wind blowing on the heath.

[*She goes into room. Lavarcham and Old Woman look at each other, then the Old Woman goes over, looks in at Deirdre through chink of the door, and then closes it carefully.*

OLD WOMAN — *in a frightened whisper.* — She's thrown off the rags she had about her, and there she is in her skin; she's putting her hair in shiny twists. Is she raving, Lavarcham, or has she a good right turning to a queen like Maeve?

LAVARCHAM — *putting up hanging very anxiously.* — It's more than raving's in her mind, or I'm the more astray; and yet she's as good a right as another, maybe, having her pleasure, though she'd spoil the world.

OLD WOMAN — *helping her.* — Be quick before she'll come back. . . . Who'd have thought we'd run before her, and she so quiet till to-night. Will the High King get the better of her, Lavarcham? If I was Conchubor, I wouldn't marry with her like at all.

LAVARCHAM. Hang that by the window. That should please her, surely. When all's said, it's her like will be the master till the end of time.

OLD WOMAN—*at the window.*—There's a mountain of blackness in the sky, and the greatest rain falling has been these long years on the earth. The gods help Conchubor. He'll be a sorry man this night, reaching his dun, and he with all his spirits, thinking to himself he'll be putting his arms around her in two days or three.

LAVARCHAM. It's more than Conchubor'll be sick and sorry, I'm thinking, before this story is told to the end.

[*Loud knocking on door at the right.*

LAVARCHAM — *startled.*— Who is that?

NAISI — *outside.*— Naisi and his brothers.

LAVARCHAM. We are lonely women. What is it you're wanting in the blackness of the night?

NAISI. We met a young girl in the woods who told us we might shelter this place if the rivers rose on the pathways and the floods gathered from the butt of the hills.

[*Old Woman clasps her hands in horror.*

LAVARCHAM — *with great alarm.*—You cannot come in. . . . There is no one let in here, and no young girl with us.

NAISI. Let us in from the great storm. Let us in and we will go further when the cloud will rise.

LAVARCHAM. Go round east to the shed and you'll have shelter. You cannot come in.

NAISI — *knocking loudly.*— Open the door or we will burst it. (*The door is shaken.*)

OLD WOMAN — *in a timid whisper.*— Let them in, and keep Deirdre in her room to-night.

· AINNLE AND ARDAR — *outside.*— Open! Open!

LAVARCHAM — *to old Woman.*— Go in and keep her.

OLD WOMAN. I couldn't keep her. I've no hold on her. Go in yourself and I will free the door.

LAVARCHAM. I must stay and turn them out. (*She pulls her hair and cloak over her face.*) Go in and keep her.

OLD WOMAN. The gods help us.

[*She runs into the inner room.*

VOICES. Open!

LAVARCHAM — *opening the door.* —

Come in then and ill-luck if you'll have it so.

[*Naisi and Ainnle and Ardan come in
and look round with astonishment.*

NAISI.   It's a rich man has this place, and
no herd at all.

LAVARCHAM — *sitting down with her
head half covered.*— It is not, and you'd best
be going quickly.

NAISI — *hilariously, shaking rain from
his clothes.*— When we've had the pick of luck
finding princely comfort in the darkness of
the night! Some rich man of Ulster should
come here and he chasing in the woods. May
we drink? (*He takes up flask.*) Whose
wine is this that we may drink his health?

LAVARCHAM.   It's no one's that you've
call to know.

NAISI.   Your own health then and length
of life. (*Pouring out wine for the three.
They drink.*)

LAVARCHAM — *very   crossly.*— You're
great boys taking a welcome where it isn't
given, and asking questions where you've no
call to. . . . If you'd a quiet place settled
up to be playing yourself, maybe, with a gentle
queen, what'd you think of young men prying
around and carrying tales? When I was a bit
of a girl the big men of Ulster had better

manners, and they the like of your three selves, in the top folly of youth. That'll be a story to tell out in Tara that Naisi is a tippler and stealer, and Ainnle the drawer of a stranger's cork.

NAISI — *quite cheerfully, sitting down beside her.*— At your age you should know there are nights when a king like Conchubor will spit upon his arm ring, and queens will stick their tongues out at the rising moon. We're that way this night, and it's not wine we're asking only. Where is the young girl told us we might shelter here?

LAVARCHAM. Asking me you'd be? We're decent people, and I wouldn't put you tracking a young girl, not if you gave me the gold clasp you have hanging on your coat.

NAISI — *giving it to her.*— Where is she?

LAVARCHAM — *in confidential whisper, putting her hand on his arm.*— Let you walk back into the hills and turn up by the second cnuceen where there are three together. You'll see a path running on the rocks and then you'll hear the dogs barking in the houses, and their noise will guide you till you come to a bit of cabin at the foot of an ash-tree. It's there there is a young and flighty girl that I'm thinking is the one you've seen.

NAISI — *hilariously.*— Here's health, then, to herself and you!

ARDAN. Here's to the years when you were young as she!

AINNLE — *in a frightened whisper.*— Naisi!

> [*Naisi looks up and Ainnle beckons to him. He goes over and Ainnle points to something on the golden mug he holds in his hand.*

NAISI — *looking at it in astonishment.*— This is the High King's. . . . I see his mark on the rim. Does Conchubor come lodging here?

LAVARCHAM — *jumping up with extreme annoyance.*— Who says it's Conchubor's? How dare young fools the like of you — (*speaking with vehement insolence*) come prying around, running the world into troubles for some slip of a girl? What brings you this place straying from Emain? (*Very bitterly.*) Though you think, maybe, young men can do their fill of foolery and there is none to blame them.

NAISI — *very soberly.*— Is the rain easing?

ARDAN. The clouds are breaking. . . . I can see Orien in the gap of the glen.

NAISI — *still cheerfully.*— Open the door

and we'll go forward to the little cabin between the ash-tree and the rocks. Lift the bolt and pull it.

> [*Deirdre comes in on left royally dressed and very beautiful. She stands for a moment, and then as the door opens she calls softly.*

DEIRDRE. Naisi! Do not leave me, Naisi. I am Deirdre of the Sorrows.

NAISI — *transfixed with amazement.*— And it is you who go around in the woods making the thrushes bear a grudge against the heavens for the sweetness of your voice singing.

DEIRDRE. It is with me you've spoken, surely. (*To Lavarcham and Old Woman.*) Take Ainnle and Ardan, these two princes, into the little hut where we eat, and serve them with what is best and sweetest. I have many things for Naisi only.

LAVARCHAM — *overawed by her tone.*— I will do it, and I ask their pardon. I have fooled them here.

DEIRDRE — *to Ainnle and Ardan.*— Do not take it badly that I am asking you to walk into our hut for a little. You will have a supper that is cooked by the cook of Conchu-

bor, and Lavarcham will tell you stories of
Maeve and Nessa and Rogh.

AINNLE.   We'll ask Lavarcham to tell us
stories of yourself, and with that we'll be well
pleased to be doing your wish.

[*They all go out except Deirdre and Naisi.*

DEIRDRE — *sitting in the high chair in
the centre.*— Come to this stool, Naisi (*pointing to the stool*).   If it's low itself the High
King would sooner be on it this night than on
the throne of Emain Macha.

NAISI — *sitting down.*— You are Fed-
limid's daughter that Conchubor has walled up
from all the men of Ulster.

DEIRDRE.   Do many know what is foretold, that Deirdre will be the ruin of the Sons
of Usna, and have a little grave by herself,
and a story will be told for ever?

NAISI.   It's a long while men have been
talking of Deirdre, the child who had all gifts,
and the beauty that has no equal; there are
many know it, and there are kings would give
a great price to be in my place this night and
you grown to a queen.   -

DEIRDRE.   It isn't many I'd call, Naisi.
. . . I was in the woods at the full moon
and I heard a voice singing.   Then I gathered
up my skirts, and I ran on a little path I have

to the verge of a rock, and I saw you pass by underneath, in your crimson cloak, singing a song, and you standing out beyond your brothers are called the Plower of Ireland.

NAISI. It's for that you called us in the dusk?

DEIRDRE — *in a low voice.* — Since that, Naisi, I have been one time the like of a ewe looking for a lamb that had been taken away from her, and one time seeing new gold on the stars, and a new face on the moon, and all times dreading Emain.

NAISI — *pulling himself together and beginning to draw back a little.* — Yet it should be a lonesome thing to be in this place and you born for great company.

DEIRDRE — *softly.* — This night I have the best company in the whole world.

NAISI — *still a little formally.* — It is I who have the best company, for when you're queen in Emain you will have none to be your match or fellow.

DEIRDRE. I will not be queen in Emain.

NAISI. Conchubor has made an oath you will, surely.

DEIRDRE. It's for that maybe I'm called Deirdre, the girl of many sorrows . . . for it's a sweet life you and I could have, Naisi.

. . . . It should be a sweet thing to have what is best and richest, if it's for a short space only.

NAISI — *very distressed.*— And we've a short space only to be triumphant and brave.

DEIRDRE.   You must not go, Naisi, and leave me to the High King, a man is ageing in his dun, with his crowds round him, and his silver and gold. (*More quickly.*) I will not live to be shut up in Emain, and wouldn't we do well paying, Naisi, with silence and a near death. (*She stands up and walks away from him.*) I'm a long while in the woods with my own self, and I'm in little dread of death, and it earned with riches would make the sun red with envy, and he going up the heavens; and the moon pale and lonesome, and she wasting away. (*She comes to him and puts her hands on his shoulders.*) Isn't it a small thing is foretold about the ruin of ourselves, Naisi, when all men have age coming and great ruin in the end?

NAISI.   Yet it's a poor thing it's I should bring you to a tale of blood and broken bodies, and the filth of the grave. . . . Wouldn't we do well to wait, Deirdre, and I each twilight meeting you on the sides of the hills?

DEIRDRE — *despondently.* — His messengers are coming.

NAISI. Messengers are coming?

DEIRDRE. To-morrow morning or the next, surely.

NAISI. Then we'll go away. It isn't I will give your like to Conchubor, not if the grave was dug to be my lodging when a week was by. (*He looks out.*) The stars are out, Deirdre, and let you come with me quickly, for it is the stars will be our lamps many nights and we abroad in Alban, and taking our journeys among the little islands in the sea. There has never been the like of the joy we'll have, Deirdre, you and I, having our fill of love at the evening and the morning till the sun is high.

DEIRDRE. And yet I'm in dread leaving this place, where I have lived always. Won't I be lonesome and I thinking on the little hill beyond, and the apple-trees do be budding in the spring-time by the post of the door? (*A little shaken by what has passed.*) Won't I be in great dread to bring you to destruction, Naisi, and you so happy and young?

NAISI. Are you thinking I'd go on living after this night, Deirdre, and you with Conchubor in Emain? Are you thinking I'd go out after hares when I've had your lips in my sight?

> [*Lavarcham comes in as they cling to each other.*

LAVARCHAM. Are you raving, Deirdre? Are you choosing this night to destroy the world?

DEIRDRE — *very deliberately.* — It's Conchubor has chosen this night calling me to Emain. (*To Naisi.*) Bring in Ainnle and Ardan, and take me from this place, where I'm in dread from this out of the footsteps of a hare passing.   [*He goes.*

DEIRDRE — *clinging to Lavarcham.* — Do not take it bad I'm going, Lavarcham. It's you have been a good friend and given me great freedom and joy, and I living on Slieve Fuadh; and maybe you'll be well pleased one day saying you have nursed Deirdre.

LAVARCHAM — *moved.* — It isn't I'll be well pleased and I far away from you. Isn't it a hard thing you're doing, but who can help it? Birds go mating in the spring of the year, and ewes at the leaves falling, but a young girl must have her lover in all the courses of the sun and moon.

DEIRDRE. Will you go to Emain in the morning?

LAVARCHAM. I will not. I'll go to Brandon in the south; and in the course of a piece, maybe, I'll be sailing back and forward on the seas to be looking on your face and the little ways you have that none can equal.

[*Naisi comes back with Ainnle and Ardan and Old Woman.*

DEIRDRE — *taking Naisi's hand.*— My two brothers, I am going with Naisi to Alban and the north to face the troubles are foretold. Will you take word to Conchubor in Emain?

AINNLE. We will go with you.

ARDAN. We will be your servants and your huntsmen, Deirdre.

DEIRDRE. It isn't one brother only of you three is brave and courteous. Will you wed us, Lavarcham? You have the words and customs.

LAVARCHAM. I will not, then. What would I want meddling in the ruin you will earn?

NAISI. Let Ainnle wed us. . . . He has been with wise men and he knows their ways.

AINNLE — *joining their hands.*— By the sun and moon and the whole earth, I wed Deirdre to Naisi. (*He steps back and holds up his hands.*) May the air bless you, and water and the wind, the sea, and all the hours of the sun and moon.

CURTAIN

ACT II.

*Alban.   Early morning in the
beginning of winter.   Outside
the tent of Deirdre and Naisi.*

ACT II

Alban. Early morning in the beginning of winter. A wood outside the tent of Deirdre and Naisi. Lavarcham comes in muffled in a cloak.

LAVARCHAM — *calling.*— Deirdre. . . . Deirdre. . . .

DEIRDRE — *coming from tent.*— My welcome, Lavarcham. . . . Whose curagh is rowing from Ulster? I saw the oars through the tops of the trees, and I thought it was you were coming towards us.

LAVARCHAM. I came in the shower was before dawn.

DEIRDRE. And who is coming?

LAVARCHAM — *mournfully.*— Let you not be startled or taking it bad, Deirdre. It's Fergus bringing messages of peace from Conchubor to take Naisi and his brother back to Emain. [*Sitting down.*

DEIRDRE — *lightly.*— Naisi and his brothers are well pleased with this place; and what yould take them back to Conchubor in Ulster?

LAVARCHAM. Their like would go any

place where they'd see death standing. (*With more agitation.*) I'm in dread Conchubor wants to have yourself and to kill Naisi, and that that'll be the ruin of the Sons of Usna. I'm silly, maybe, to be dreading the like, but those have a great love for yourself have a right to be in dread always.

DEIRDRE — *more   anxiously.* — Emain should be no safe place for myself and Naisi. And isn't it a hard thing they'll leave us no peace, Lavarcham, and we so quiet in the woods?

LAVARCHAM — *impressively.*— It's a hard thing, surely; but let you take my word and swear Naisi, by the earth, and the sun over it, and the four quarters of the moon, he'll not go back to Emain — for good faith or bad faith — the time Conchubor's keeping the high throne of Ireland. . . . . It's that would save you, surely.

DEIRDRE — *without hope.*— There's little power in oaths to stop what's coming, and little power in what I'd do, Lavarcham, to change the story of Conchubor and Naisi and the things old men foretold.

LAVARCHAM — *aggressively.* — W a s there little power in what you did the night you dressed in your finery and ran Naisi off along with you, in spite of Conchubor and the big nobles did dread the blackness of your luck? It was power enough you had that night to bring distress and anguish; and now I'm pointing you a way to save Naisi, you'll not stir stick or straw to aid me.

DEIRDRE — *a little haughtily.*— Let you not raise your voice against me, Lavarcham, if you have will itself to guard Naisi.

LAVARCHAM — *breaking out in anger.* — Naisi is it? I didn't care if the crows were stripping his thigh-bones at the dawn of day. It's to stop your own despair and wailing, and you waking up in a cold bed, without the man you have your heart on, I am raging now. (*Starting up with temper.*) Yet there is more men than Naisi in it; and maybe I was a big fool thinking his dangers, and this day, would fill you up with dread.

DEIRDRE — *sharply.*— Let you end; such talking is a fool's only, when it's well you know if a thing harmed Naisi it isn't I would live after him. (*With distress.*) It's well you know it's this day I'm dreading seven years, and I fine nights watching the heifers walking to the haggard with long shadows on the grass; (*with emotion*) or the time I've been stretched in the sunshine, when I've heard

Ainnle and Ardan stepping lightly, and they saying: Was there ever the like of Deirdre for a happy and sleepy queen?

LAVARCHAM — *not fully pacified.* — And yet you'll go, and welcome is it, if Naisi chooses?

DEIRDRE. I've dread going or staying, Lavarcham. It's lonesome this place, having happiness like ours, till I'm asking each day will this day match yesterday, and will to-morrow take a good place beside the same day in the year that's gone, and wondering all times is it a game worth playing, living on until you're dried and old, and our joy is gone for ever.

LAVARCHAM. If it's that ails you, I tell you there's little hurt getting old, though young girls and poets do be storming at the shapes of age. (*Passionately.*) There's little hurt getting old, saving when you're looking back, the way I'm looking this day, and seeing the young you have a love for breaking up their hearts with folly. (*Going to Deirdre.*) Take my word and stop Naisi, and the day'll come you'll have more joy having the senses of an old woman and you with your little grandsons shrieking round you, than I'd have this night putting on the red mouth and the white arms you have, to go walking lonesome byeways with a gamey king.

DEIRDRE. It's little joy of a young woman, or an old woman, I'll have from this day, surely. But what use is in our talking when there's Naisi on the foreshore, and Fergus with him?

LAVARCHAM — *despairingly.*— I'm late so with my warnings, for Fergus'd talk the moon over to take a new path in the sky. (*With reproach.*) You'll not stop him this day, and isn't it a strange story you were a plague and torment, since you were that height, to those did hang their lifetimes on your voice. (*Overcome with trouble; gathering her cloak about her.*) Don't think bad of my crying. I'm not the like of many and I'd see a score of naked corpses and not heed them at all, but I'm destroyed seeing yourself in your hour of joy when the end is coming surely.

[*Owen comes in quickly, rather ragged, bows to Deirdre.*

OWEN — *to Lavarcham.*— Fergus's men are calling you. You were seen on the path, and he and Naisi want you for their talk below.

LAVARCHAM — *looking at him with dislike.*— Yourself's an ill-lucky thing to meet a

morning is the like of this. Yet if you are a
spy itself I'll go and give my word that's
wanting surely.   [*Goes out.*

OWEN — *to Deirdre.*— So I've found you
alone, and I after waiting three weeks getting
ague and asthma in the chill of the bogs, till
I saw Naisi caught with Fergus.

DEIRDRE. I've heard news of Fergus;
what brought you from Ulster?

OWEN — *who has been searching, finds
a loaf and sits down eating greedily, and cut-
ting it with a large knife.*— The full moon,
I'm thinking, and it squeezing the crack in my
skull. Was there ever a man crossed nine
waves after a fool's wife and he not away in
his head?

DEIRDRE — *absently.*— It should be a
long time since you left Emain, where there's
civility in speech with queens.

OWEN. It's a long while, surely. It's
three weeks I am losing my manners beside
the Saxon bull-frogs at the head of the bog.
Three weeks is a long space, and yet you're
seven years spancelled with Naisi and the pair.

DEIRDRE — *beginning to fold up her silks
and jewels.*— Three weeks of your days might
be long, surely, yet seven years are a short
space for the like of Naisi and myself.

OWEN — *derisively.* — If they're a short
space there aren't many the like of you.
Wasn't there a queen in Tara had to walk out
every morning till she'd meet a stranger and
see the flame of courtship leaping up within
his eye? Tell me now, (*leaning towards her*)
are you well pleased that length with the same
man snorting next you at the dawn of day?

DEIRDRE — *very quietly.* — Am I well
pleased seven years seeing the same sun throwing light across the branches at the dawn of
day? It's a heartbreak to the wise that it's for
a short space we have the same things only.
(*With contempt.*) Yet the earth itself is a
silly place, maybe, when a man's a fool and
talker.

OWEN — *sharply.* — Well, go, take your
choice. Stay here and rot with Naisi or go to
Conchubor in Emain. Conchubor's a wrinkled
fool with a swelling belly on him, and eyes
falling downward from his shining crown;
Naisi should be stale and weary. Yet there
are many roads, Deirdre, and I tell you I'd
leifer be bleaching in a bog-hole than living
on without a touch of kindness from your eyes
and voice. It's a poor thing to be so lonesome
you'd squeeze kisses on a cur dog's nose.

DEIRDRE. Are there no women like

yourself could be your friends in Emain?

OWEN — *vehemently.* — There are none like you, Deirdre. It's for that I'm asking are you going back this night with Fergus?

DEIRDRE.   I will go where Naisi chooses.

OWEN — *with a burst of rage.* — It's Naisi, Naisi, is it? Then, I tell you, you'll have great sport one day seeing Naisi getting a harshness in his two sheep's eyes and he looking on yourself. Would you credit it, my father used to be in the broom and heather kissing Lavarcham, with a little bird chirping out above their heads, and now she'd scare a raven from a carcase on a hill. (*With a sad cry that brings dignity into his voice.*) Queens get old, Deirdre, with their white and long arms going from them, and their backs hooping. I tell you it's a poor thing to see a queen's nose reaching down to scrape her chin.

DEIRDRE — *looking out, a little uneasy.* — Naisi and Fergus are coming on the path.

OWEN.   I'll go so, for if I had you seven years I'd be jealous of the midges and the dust is in the air. (*Muffles himself in his cloak; with a sort of warning in his voice.*) I'll give you a riddle, Deirdre: Why isn't my father as ugly and old as Conchubor? You've no answer? . . . . It's because Naisi killed him.

(*With curious expression.*)   Think of that
and you awake at night, hearing Naisi snor-
ing, or the night you hear strange stories of
the things I'm doing in Alban or in Ulster
either.

> [*He goes out, and in a moment Naisi and
> Fergus come in on the other side.*

NAISI — *gaily.*— Fergus has brought messages of peace from Conchubor.

DEIRDRE — *greeting Fergus.*— He is
welcome.   Let you rest, Fergus, you should be
hot and thirsty after mounting the rocks.

FERGUS.   It's a sunny nook you've found
in Alban; yet any man would be well pleased
mounting higher rocks to fetch yourself and
Naisi back to Emain.

DEIRDRE — *with keenness.* — They've
answered?   They would go?

FERGUS — *benignly.*— They have not,
but when I was a young man we'd have given
a lifetime to be in Ireland a score of weeks;
and to this day the old men have nothing so
heavy as knowing it's in a short while they'll
lose the high skies are over Ireland, and the
lonesome mornings with birds crying on the
bogs.   Let you come this day, for there's no
place but Ireland where the Gael can have
peace always.

NAISI — *gruffly.*— It's true, surely. Yet we're better this place while Conchubor's in Emain Macha.

FERGUS — *giving him parchments.*— There are your sureties and Conchubor's seal. (*To Deirdre.*) I am your surety with Conchubor. You'll not be young always, and it's time you were making yourselves ready for the years will come, building up a homely dun beside the seas of Ireland, and getting in your children from the princes' wives. It's little joy wandering till age is on you and your youth is gone away, so you'd best come this night, for you'd have great pleasure putting out your foot and saying, " I am in Ireland, surely."

DEIRDRE. It isn't pleasure I'd have while Conchubor is king in Emain.

FERGUS — *almost annoyed.*— Would you doubt the seals of Conal Cearneach and the kings of Meath? (*He gets parchments from his cloak and gives them to Naisi. More gently.*) It's easy being fearful and you alone in the woods, yet it would be a poor thing if a timid woman (*taunting her a little*) could turn away the Sons of Usna from the life of kings. Let you be thinking on the years to come, Deirdre, and the way you'd have a right to see Naisi a high and white-haired justice beside some king of Emain. Wouldn't it be a poor story if a queen the like of you should have no thought but to be scraping up her hours dallying in the sunshine with the sons of kings?

DEIRDRE — *turning away a little haughtily.*— I leave the choice to Naisi. (*Turning back towards Fergus.*) Yet you'd do well, Fergus, to go on your own way, for the sake of your own years, so you'll not be saying till your hour of death, maybe, it was yourself brought Naisi and his brothers to a grave was scooped by treachery. [*Goes into tent.*

FERGUS. It is a poor thing to see a queen so lonesome and afraid. (*He watches till he is sure Deirdre cannot hear him.*) Listen now to what I'm saying. You'd do well to come back to men and women are your match and comrades, and not be lingering until the day that you'll grow weary, and hurt Deirdre showing her the hardness will grow up within your eyes. . . . You're here years and plenty to know it's truth I'm saying.

> [*Deirdre comes out of tent with a horn of wine, she catches the beginning of Naisi's speech and stops with stony wonder.*

NAISI — *very thoughtfully.*— I'll not tell you a lie. There have been days a while past when I've been throwing a line for salmon or watching for the run of hares, that I've a dread upon me a day'd come I'd weary of her voice, (*very slowly*) and Deirdre'd see I'd wearied.

FERGUS — *sympathetic but triumphant.*— I knew it, Naisi. . . . And take my word, Deirdre's seen your dread and she'll have no peace from this out in the woods.

NAISI — *with confidence.*— She's not seen it. . . . Deirdre's no thought of getting old or wearied; it's that puts wonder in her ways, and she with spirits would keep bravery and laughter in a town with plague.

[*Deirdre drops the horn of wine and crouches down where she is.*

FERGUS. That humour'll leave her. But we've no call going too far, with one word borrowing another. Will you come this night to Emain Macha?

NAISI. I'll not go, Fergus. I've had dreams of getting old and weary, and losing my delight in Deirdre; but my dreams were dreams only. What are Conchubor's seals and all your talk of Emain and the fools of Meath beside one evening in Glen Masain? We'll stay this place till our lives and time are

worn out. It's that word you may take in
your curagh to Conchubor in Emain.

FERGUS — *gathering up his parchments.*
— And you won't go, surely.

NAISI. I will not. . . . I've had dread,
I tell you, dread winter and summer, and the
autumn and the springtime, even when there's
a bird in every bush making his own stir till
the fall of night; but this talk's brought me
ease, and I see we're as happy as the leaves on
the young trees, and we'll be so ever and
always, though we'd live the age of the eagle
and the salmon and the crow of Britain.

FERGUS — *with anger.*— Where are your
brothers? My message is for them also.

NAISI. You'll see them above chasing
otters by the stream.

FERGUS — *bitterly.*— It isn't much I was
mistaken, thinking you were hunters only.

[*He goes, Naisi turns towards tent
and sees Deirdre crouching down with
her cloak round her face. Deirdre
comes out.*

NAISI. You've heard my words to
Fergus? (*She does not answer. A pause. He
puts his arm round her.*) Leave troubling,
and we'll go this night to Glen da Ruadh,

where the salmon will be running with the tide. [*Crosses and sits down.*

DEIRDRE — *in a very low voice.*— With the tide in a little while we will be journeying again, or it is our own blood maybe will be running away. (*She turns and clings to him.*) The dawn and evening are a little while, the winter and the summer pass quickly, and what way would you and I, Naisi, have joy for ever?

NAISI. We'll have the joy is highest till our age is come, for it isn't Fergus's talk of great deeds could take us back to Emain.

DEIRDRE. It isn't to great deeds you're going but to near troubles, and the shortening of your days the time that they are bright and sunny; and isn't it a poor thing that I, Deirdre, could not hold you away?

NAISI. I've said we'd stay in Alban always.

DEIRDRE. There's no place to stay always. . . . It's a long time we've had, pressing the lips together, going up and down, resting in our arms, Naisi, waking with the smell of June in the tops of the grasses, and listening to the birds in the branches that are highest. . . . It's a long time we've had, but the end has come, surely.

NAISI.   Would you have us go to Emain, though if any ask the reason we do not know it, and we journeying as the thrushes come from the north, or young birds fly out on a dark sea?

DEIRDRE. (There's reason all times for an end that's come.) And I'm well pleased, Naisi, we're going forward in the winter the time the sun has a low place, and the moon has her mastery in a dark sky, for it's you and I are well lodged our last day, where there is a light behind the clear trees, and the berries on the thorns are a red wall.

NAISI.   If our time in this place is ended, come away without Ainnle and Ardan to the woods of the east, for it's right to be away from all people when two lovers have their love only.   Come away and we'll be safe always.

DEIRDRE—*broken-hearted.*— There's no safe place, Naisi, on the ridge of the world. . . . . And it's in the quiet woods I've seen them digging our grave, throwing out the clay on leaves are bright and withered.

NAISI — *still more eagerly.*— Come away, Deirdre, and it's little we'll think of safety or the grave beyond it, and we resting in a little corner between the daytime and the long night.

DEIRDRE — *clearly and gravely.*— It's this hour we're between the daytime and a night where there is sleep for ever, and isn't it a better thing to be following on to a near death, than to be bending the head down, and dragging with the feet, and seeing one day a blight showing upon love where it is sweet and tender.

NAISI — *his voice broken with distraction.*— If a near death is coming what will be my trouble losing the earth and the stars over it, and you, Deirdre, are their flame and bright crown? Come away into the safety of the woods.

DEIRDRE — *shaking her head slowly.*— There are as many ways to wither love as there are stars in a night of Samhain; but there is no way to keep life, or love with it, a short space only. . . . It's for that there's nothing lonesome like a love is watching out the time most lovers do be sleeping. . . . It's for that we're setting out for Emain Macha when the tide turns on the sand.

NAISI — *giving in.*— You're right, maybe. It should be a poor thing to see great lovers and they sleepy and old.

DEIRDRE — *with a more tender intensity.* —We're seven years without roughness or growing weary; seven years so sweet and shining, the gods would be hard set to give us seven days the like of them. It's for that we're going to Emain, where there'll be a rest for ever, or a place for forgetting, in great crowds and they making a stir.

NAISI — *very softly.*— We'll go, surely, in place of keeping a watch on a love had no match and it wasting away. (*They cling to each other for a moment, then Naisi looks up.*) There are Fergus and Lavarcham and my two brothers.

[*Deirdre goes. Naisi sits with his head bowed. Owen runs in stealthily, comes behind Naisi and seizes him round the arms. Naisi shakes him off and whips out his sword.*

OWEN — *screaming with derisive laughter and showing his empty hands.*— Ah, Naisi, wasn't it well I didn't kill you that time? There was a fright you got! I've been watching Fergus above — don't be frightened — and I've come down to see him getting the cold shoulder, and going off alone.

[*Fergus and others come in. They are all subdued like men at a queen's wake.*

NAISI — *putting up his sword.*— There

he is. (*Goes to Fergus.*) We are going back when the tide turns, I and Deirdre with yourself.

ALL. Going back!

AINNLE. And you'll end your life with Deirdre, though she has no match for keeping spirits in a little company is far away by itself?

ARDAN. It's seven years myself and Ainnle have been servants and bachelors for yourself and Deirdre. Why will you take her back to Conchubor?

NAISI. I have done what Deirdre wishes and has chosen.

FERGUS. You've made a choice wise men will be glad of in the five ends of Ireland.

OWEN. Wise men is it, and they going back to Conchubor? I could stop them only Naisi put in his sword among my father's ribs, and when a man's done that he'll not credit your oath. Going to Conchubor! I could tell of plots and tricks, and spies were well paid for their play. (*He throws up a bag of gold.*) Are you paid, Fergus?

[*He scatters gold pieces over Fergus.*

FERGUS. He is raving. . . . Seize him.

OWEN — *flying between them.* — You won't. Let the lot of you be off to Emain, but I'll be off before you. . . . Dead men, dead men! Men who'll die for Deirdre's beauty; I'll be before you in the grave!

[*Runs out with his knife in his hand. They all run after him except Lavarcham, who looks out and then clasps her hands. Deirdre comes out to her in a dark cloak.*

DEIRDRE. What has happened?

LAVARCHAM. It's Owen's gone raging mad, and he's after splitting his gullet beyond at the butt of the stone. There was ill luck this day in his eye. And he knew a power if he'd said it all.

[*Naisi comes back quickly, followed by the others.*

AINNLE — *coming in very excited.*— That man knew plots of Conchubor's. We'll not go to Emain, where Conchubor may love her and have hatred for yourself.

FERGUS. Would you mind a fool and raver?

AINNLE. It's many times there's more sense in madmen than the wise. We will not obey Conchubor.

NAISI. I and Deirdre have chosen; we will go back with Fergus.

ARDAN. We will not go back. We will burn your curaghs by the sea.

FERGUS. My sons and I will guard them.

AINNLE. We will blow the horn of Usna and our friends will come to aid us.

NAISI. It is my friends will come.

AINNLE. Your friends will bind your hands, and you out of your wits.

[*Deirdre comes forward quickly and comes between Ainnle and Naisi.*

DEIRDRE — *in a low voice.*— For seven years the Sons of Usna have not raised their voices in a quarrel.

AINNLE. We will not take you to Emain.

ARDAN. It is Conchubor has broken our peace.

AINNLE — *to Deirdre.*— Stop Naisi going. What way would we live if Conchubor should take you from us?

DEIRDRE. There is no one could take me from you. I have chosen to go back with Fergus. Will you quarrel with me, Ainnle, though I have been your queen these seven years in Alban?

AINNLE — *subsiding suddenly.* — Naisi has no call to take you.

ARDAN. Why are you going?

DEIRDRE — *to both of them and the*

others.— It is my wish. . . . It may be I will not have Naisi growing an old man in Alban with an old woman at his side, and young girls pointing out and saying, " that is Deirdre and Naisi had great beauty in their youth." It may be we do well putting a sharp end to the day is brave and glorious, as our fathers put a sharp end to the days of the kings of Ireland; or that I'm wishing to set my foot on Slieve Fuadh, where I was running one time and leaping the streams, (*to Lavarcham*) and that I'd be well pleased to see our little apple-trees, Lavarcham, behind our cabin on the hill; or that I've learned, Fergus, it's a lonesome thing to be away from Ireland always.

AINNLE — *giving in.*— There is no place but will be lonesome to us from this out, and we thinking on our seven years in Alban.

DEIRDRE — *to Naisi.*— It's in this place we'd be lonesome in the end. . . . Take down Fergus to the sea. He has been a guest had a hard welcome and he bringing messages of peace.

FERGUS. We will make your curagh ready and it fitted for the voyage of a king.

[*He goes with Naisi.*

DEIRDRE. Take your spears, Ainnle and Adran, and go down before me, and take your horse-boys to be carrying my cloaks are on the threshold.

AINNLE — *obeying.*— It's with a poor heart we'll carry your things this day we have carried merrily so often, and we hungry and cold.

[*They gather up things and go out.*

DEIRDRE — *to Lavarcham.*— Go you, too, Lavarcham. You are old, and I will follow quickly.

LAVARCHAM. I'm old, surely, and the hopes I had my pride in are broken and torn.

[*She goes out, with a look of awe at Deirdre.*

DEIRDRE — *clasping her hands.*— Woods of Cuan, woods of Cuan, dear country of the east! It's seven years we've had a life was joy only, and this day we're going west, this day we're facing death, maybe, and death should be a poor, untidy thing, though it's a queen that dies.

[*She goes out slowly.*

CURTAIN

ACT III.

Tent below Emain Macha.

ACT III

Tent below Emain, with shabby skins and benches. There is an opening at each side and at back, the latter closed. Old Woman comes in with food and fruits and arranges them on table. Conchubor comes in on right.

CONCHUBOR — *sharply.*— Has no one come with news for me?

OLD WOMAN. I've seen no one at all, Conchubor.

CONCHUBOR — *watches her working for a moment, then makes sure opening at back is closed.*— Go up then to Emain, you're not wanting here. (*A noise heard left.*) Who is that?

OLD WOMAN — *going left.*— It's Lavarcham coming again. She's a great wonder for jogging back and forward through the world, and I made certain she'd be off to meet them; but she's coming alone, Conchubor, my dear child Deirdre isn't with her at all.

CONCHUBOR. Go up so and leave us.

OLD WOMAN — *pleadingly.*— I'd be well pleased to set my eyes on Deirdre if she's coming this night, as we're told.

CONCHUBOR — *impatiently.*— It's   not
long till you'll see her.   But I've matters with
Lavarcham, and let you go now, I'm saying.

[*He shows her out right, as Lavarcham
comes in on the left.*

LAVARCHAM — *looking round her with
suspicion.*— This is a queer place to find you,
and it's a queer place to be lodging Naisi and
his brothers, and Deirdre with them, and the
lot of us tired out with the long way we have
been walking.

CONCHUBOR.   You've come along with
them the whole journey?

LAVARCHAM.   I   have,   then,   though
I've no call now to be wandering that length
to a wedding or a burial, or the two together.
(*She sits down wearily.*)   It's a poor thing
the way me and you is getting old, Conchubor,
and I'm thinking you yourself have no call to
be loitering this place getting your death, maybe, in the cold of night.

CONCHUBOR.   I'm waiting only to know
is Fergus stopped in the north.

LAVARCHAM — *more   sharply.* — He's
stopped, surely, and that's a trick has me
thinking you have it in mind to bring trouble
this night on Emain and Ireland and the big
world's east beyond them.   (*She goes to him.*)

And yet you'd do well to be going to your dun, and not putting shame on her meeting the High King, and she seamed and sweaty and in great disorder from the dust of many roads. (*Laughing derisively.*) Ah, Conchubor, my lad, beauty goes quickly in the woods, and you'd let a great gasp, I tell you, if you set your eyes this night on Deirdre.

CONCHUBOR — *fiercely.*— It's little I care if she's white and worn, for it's I did rear her from a child. I should have a good right to meet and see her always.

LAVARCHAM. A good right is it? Haven't the blind a good right to be seeing, and the lame to be dancing, and the dummies singing tunes? It's that right you have to be looking for gaiety on Deirdre's lips. (*Coaxingly.*) Come on to your dun, I'm saying, and leave her quiet for one night itself.

CONCHUBOR — *with sudden anger.*— I'll not go, when it's long enough I am above in my dun stretching east and west without a comrade, and I more needy, maybe, than the thieves of Meath. . . . You think I'm old and wise, but I tell you the wise know the old must die, and they'll leave no chance for a thing slipping from them they've set their blood to win.

LAVARCHAM — *nodding her head.*— If you're old and wise, it's I'm the same, Conchubor, and I'm telling you you'll not have her though you're ready to destroy mankind and skin the gods to win her. There's things a king can't have, Conchubor, and if you go rampaging this night you'll be apt to win nothing but death for many, and a sloppy face of trouble on your own self before the day will come.

CONCHUBOR. It's too much talk you have. (*Goes right.*) Where is Owen? Did you see him no place and you coming the road?

LAVARCHAM. I seen him surely. He went spying on Naisi, and now the worms is spying on his own inside.

CONCHUBOR—*exultingly.*— Naisi killed him?

LAVARCHAM. He did not, then. It was Owen destroyed himself running mad because of Deirdre. Fools and kings and scholars are all one in a story with her like, and Owen thought he'd be a great man, being the first corpse in the game you'll play this night in Emain.

CONCHUBOR. It's yourself should be the first corpse, but my other messengers are coming, men from the clans that hated Usna.

LAVARCHAM — *drawing back hopelessly.*— Then the gods have pity on us all!

[*Men with weapons come in.*

CONCHUBOR — *to Soldiers.*— Are Ainnle and Ardan separate from Naisi?

MEN. They are, Conchubor. We've got them off, saying they were needed to make ready Deirdre's house.

CONCHUBOR. And Naisi and Deirdre are coming?

SOLDIER. Naisi's coming, surely, and a woman with him is putting out the glory of the moon is rising and the sun is going down.

CONCHUBOR — *looking at Lavarcham.* — That's your story that she's seamed and ugly?

SOLDIER. I have more news. (*Pointing to Lavarcham.*) When that woman heard you were bringing Naisi this place, she sent a horse-boy to call Fergus from the north.

CONCHUBOR — *to Lavarcham.*— It's for that you've been playing your tricks, but what you've won is a nearer death for Naisi. (*To Soldiers.*) Go up and call my fighters, and take that woman up to Emain.

LAVARCHAM. I'd liefer stay this place. I've done my best, but if a bad end is coming, surely it would be a good thing maybe I was here to tend her.

CONCHUBOR — *fiercely.*— Take her to Emain; it's too many tricks she's tried this day already. (*A Soldier goes to her.*)

LAVARCHAM. Don't touch me. (*She puts her cloak round her and catches Conchubor's arm.*) I thought to stay your hand with my stories till Fergus would come to be beside them, the way I'd save yourself, Conchubor, and Naisi and Emain Macha; but I'll walk up now into your halls, and I'll say (*with a gesture*) it's here nettles will be growing, and beyond thistles and docks. I'll go into your high chambers, where you've been figuring yourself stretching out your neck for the kisses of a queen of women; and I'll say it's here there'll be deer stirring and goats scratching, and sheep waking and coughing when there is a great wind from the north. (*Shaking herself loose. Conchubor makes a sign to Soldiers.*) I'm going, surely. In a short space I'll be sitting up with many listening to the flames crackling, and the beams breaking, and I looking on the great blaze will be the end of Emain.   [*She goes out.*

CONCHUBOR — *looking out.*— I see two people in the trees; it should be Naisi and

Deirdre. (*To Soldier.*)   Let you tell them they'll lodge here tonight.

[*Conchubor goes out right. Naisi and Deirdre come in on left, very weary.*

NAISI — *to Soldiers.*— Is it this place he's made ready for myself and Deirdre?

SOLDIER. The Red Branch House is being aired and swept and you'll be called there when a space is by; till then you'd find fruits and drink on this table, and so the gods be with you.   [*Goes out right.*

NAISI — *looking round.*— It's a strange place he's put us camping and we come back as his friends.

DEIRDRE.   He's likely making up a welcome for us, having curtains shaken out and rich rooms put in order; and it's right he'd have great state to meet us, and you his sister's son.

NAISI — *gloomily.*— It's little we want with state or rich rooms or curtains, when we're used to the ferns only and cold streams and they making a stir.

DEIRDRE — *roaming round room.*— We want what is our right in Emain (*looking at hangings*), and though he's riches in store for us it's a shabby, ragged place he's put us waiting, with frayed rugs and skins are eaten by the moths.

NAISI — *a little impatiently.*— There are few would worry over skins and moths on this first night that we've come back to Emain.

DEIRDRE — *brightly.*— You should be well pleased it's for that I'd worry all times, when it's I have kept your tent these seven years as tidy as a bee-hive or a linnet's nest. If Conchubor'd a queen like me in Emain he'd not have stretched these rags to meet us. (*She pulls hanging, and it opens.*) There's new earth on the ground and a trench dug. . . . It's a grave, Naisi, that is wide and deep.

NAISI — *goes over and pulls back curtain showing grave.*— And that'll be our home in Emain. . . . He's dug it wisely at the butt of a hill, with fallen trees to hide it. He'll want to have us killed and buried before Fergus comes.

DEIRDRE. Take me away. . . . Take me to hide in the rocks, for the night is coming quickly.

NAISI — *pulling himself together.*— I will not leave my brothers.

DEIRDRE — *vehemently.*— It's of us two he's jealous. Come away to the places where we're used to have our company. . . .

Wouldn't it be a good thing to lie hid in the high ferns together? (*She pulls him left.*) I hear strange words in the trees.

NAISI. It should be the strange fighters of Conchubor. I saw them passing as we came.

DEIRDRE — *pulling him towards the right.*— Come to this side. Listen, Naisi!

NAISI. There are more of them. . . . We are shut in, and I have not Ainnle and Ardan to stand near me. Isn't it a hard thing that we three who have conquered many may not die together?

DEIRDRE — *sinking down.*— And isn't it a hard thing that you and I are in this place by our opened grave; though none have lived had happiness like ours those days in Alban that went by so quick.

NAISI. It's a hard thing, surely, we've lost those days for ever; and yet it's a good thing, maybe, that all goes quick, for when I'm in that grave it's soon a day'll come you'll be too wearied to be crying out, and that day'll bring you ease.

DEIRDRE. I'll not be here to know if that is true.

NAISI. It's our three selves he'll kill to-night, and then in two months or three you'll

see him walking down for courtship with
yourself.

DEIRDRE.   I'll not be here.

NAISI — *hard.*— You'd best keep him off,
maybe, and then, when the time comes, make
your way to some place west in Donegal, and
it's there you'll get used to stretching out
lonesome at the fall of night, and waking lonesome for the day.

DEIRDRE.   Let you not be saying things
are worse than death.

NAISI — *a little recklessly.*— I've one
word left. If a day comes in the west that the
larks are cocking their crests on the edge of
the clouds, and the cuckoos making a stir, and
there's a man you'd fancy, let you not be
thinking that day I'd be well pleased you'd go
on keening always.

DEIRDRE — *turning to look at him.*—
And if it was I that died, Naisi, would you
take another woman to fill up my place?

NAISI — *very mournfully.*— It's little I
know, saving only that it's a hard and bitter
thing leaving the earth, and a worse and
harder thing leaving yourself alone and desolate to be making lamentation on its face
always.

DEIRDRE.   I'll die when you do, Naisi.

I'd not have come here from Alban but I knew I'd be along with you in Emain, and you living or dead. . . . Yet this night it's strange and distant talk you're making only.

NAISI. There's nothing, surely, the like of a new grave of open earth for putting a great space between two friends that love.

DEIRDRE. If there isn't, it's that grave when it's closed will make us one for ever, and we two lovers have had great space without weariness or growing old or any sadness of the mind.

CONCHUBOR — *coming in on right.*— I'd bid you welcome, Naisi.

NAISI — *standing up.*— You're welcome, Conchubor. I'm well pleased you've come.

CONCHUBOR — *blandly.*— Let you not think bad of this place where I've put you till other rooms are readied.

NAISI — *breaking out.*— We know the room you've readied. We know what stirred you to send your seals and Fergus into Alban and stop him in the north, (*opening curtain and pointing to the grave*) and dig that grave before us. Now I ask what brought you here?

CONCHUBOR. I've come to look on Deirdre.

NAISI. Look on her. You're a knacky

fancier, and it's well you chose the one you'd lure from Alban. Look on her, I tell you, and when you've looked I've got ten fingers will squeeze your mottled goose neck, though you're king itself.

DEIRDRE — *coming between them.*— Hush, Naisi! Maybe Conchubor'll make peace. . . . Do not mind him, Conchubor; he has cause to rage.

CONCHUBOR. It's little I heed his raging, when a call would bring my fighters from the trees. . . . But what do you say, Deirdre?

DEIRDRE. I'll say so near that grave we seem three lonesome people, and by a new made grave there's no man will keep brooding on a woman's lips, or on the man he hates. It's not long till your own grave will be dug in Emain, and you'd go down to it more easy if you'd let call Ainnle and Ardan, the way we'd have a supper all together, and fill that grave, and you'll be well pleased from this out, having four new friends the like of us in Emain.

CONCHUBOR — *looking at her for a moment.*— That's the first friendly word I've heard you speaking, Deirdre. A game the like of yours should be the proper thing for softening the heart and putting sweetness in the

tongue; and yet this night when I hear you
I've small blame left for Naisi that he stole
you off from Ulster.

DEIRDRE — *to   Naisi.*— Now,   Naisi,
answer gently, and we'll be friends to-night.

NAISI — *doggedly.*— I have no call but to
be friendly. I'll answer what you will.

DEIRDRE — *taking Naisi's hand.*— Then
you'll call Conchubor your friend and king,
the man who reared me up upon Slieve Fuadh.

[*As Conchubor is going to clasp Naisi's
     hand cries are heard behind.*

CONCHUBOR.   What noise is that?

AINNLE — *behind.*— Naisi. . . . Naisi
Come to us; we are betrayed and broken.

NAISI.   It's Ainnle crying out in a battle.

CONCHUBOR.   I   was   near   won   this
night, but death's between us now.

[*He goes out.*

DEIRDRE — *clinging to Naisi.*— There is
no battle. . . . Do not leave me, Naisi.

NAISI.   I must go to them.

DEIDRE — *beseechingly.*— Do   not   leave
me, Naisi. Let us creep up in the darkness
behind the grave. If there's a battle, maybe
the strange fighters will be destroyed, when
Ainnle and Ardan are against them.

[*Cries heard.*

NAISI — *wildly*.— I hear Ardan crying out. Do not hold me from my brothers.

DEIRDRE. Do not leave me, Naisi. Do not leave me broken and alone.

NAISI. I cannot leave my brothers when it is I who have defied the king.

DEIRDRE. I will go with you.

NAISI. You cannot come. Do not hold me from the fight.

[*He throws her aside almost roughly.*

DEIRDRE — *with restraint*.— Go to your brothers. For seven years you have been kindly, but the hardness of death has come between us.

NAISI — *looking at her aghast*.— And you'll have me meet death with a hard word from your lips in my ear?

DEIRDRE. We've had a dream, but this night has waked us surely. In a little while we've lived too long, Naisi, and isn't it a poor thing we should miss the safety of the grave, and we trampling its edge?

AINNLE — *behind*.— Naisi, Naisi, we are attacked and ruined!

DEIRDRE. Let you go where they are calling. (*She looks at him for an instant coldly.*) Have you no shame loitering and talking, and a cruel death facing Ainnle and Ardan in the woods?

NAISI — *frantic.* — They'll not get a death that's cruel, and they with men alone. It's women that have loved are cruel only; and if I went on living from this day I'd be putting a curse on the lot of them I'd meet walking in the east or west, putting a curse on the sun that gave them beauty, and on the madder and the stone-crop put red upon their cloaks.

DEIRDRE — *bitterly.* — I'm well pleased there's no one in this place to make a story that Naisi was a laughing-stock the night he died.

NAISI. There'd not be many'd make a story, for that mockery is in your eyes this night will spot the face of Emain with a plague of pitted graves.   [*He goes out.*

CONCHUBOR — *outside.* — That is Naisi. Strike him! (*Tumult. Deirdre crouches down on Naisi's cloak. Conchubor comes in hurriedly.*) They've met their death — the three that stole you, Deirdre, and from this out you'll be my queen in Emain.

[*A keen of men's voices is heard behind.*

DEIRDRE — *bewildered and terrified.* — It is not I will be a queen.

CONCHUBOR. Make your lamentation a short while if you will, but it isn't long till

a day'll come when you begin pitying a man
is old and desolate, and High King also. . . .
Let you not fear me, for it's I'm well pleased
you have a store of pity for the three that were
your friends in Alban.

DEIRDRE. I have pity, surely. . . . It's
the way pity has me this night, when I think
of Naisi, that I could set my teeth into the
heart of a king.

CONCHUBOR. I know well pity's cruel,
when it was my pity for my own self destroyed
Naisi.

DEIRDRE — *more wildly.*— It was my
words without pity gave Naisi a death will
have no match until the ends of life and time.
(*Breaking out into a keen.*) But who'll pity
Deirdre has lost the lips of Naisi from her
neck and from her cheek for ever? Who'll
pity Deirdre has lost the twilight in the woods
with Naisi, when beech-trees were silver and
copper, and ash-trees were fine gold?

CONCHUBOR — *bewildered.* — It's   I'll
know the way to pity and care you, and I with
a share of troubles has me thinking this night
it would be a good bargain if it was I was in
the grave, and Deirdre crying over me, and
it was Naisi who was old and desolate.

[*Keen heard.*

DEIRDRE — *wild with sorrow.* — It is I who am desolate; I, Deirdre, that will not live till I am old.

CONCHUBOR. It's not long you'll be desolate, and I seven years saying, " It's a bright day for Deirdre in the woods of Alban "; or saying again, " What way will Deirdre be sleeping this night, and wet leaves and branches driving from the north? " Let you not break the thing I've set my life on, and you giving yourself up to your sorrow when it's joy and sorrow do burn out like straw blazing in an east wind.

DEIRDRE — *turning on him.* — Was it that way with your sorrow, when I and Naisi went northward from Slieve Fuadh and let raise our sails for Alban?

CONCHUBOR. There's one sorrow has no end surely — that's being old and lonesome. (*With extraordinary pleading.*) But you and I will have a little peace in Emain, with harps playing, and old men telling stories at the fall of night. I've let build rooms for our two selves, Deirdre, with red gold upon the walls and ceilings that are set with bronze. There was never a queen in the east had a house the like of your house, that's waiting for yourself in Emain.

SOLDIER — *running in.*— Emain is in flames. Fergus has come back and is setting fire to the world. Come up, Conchubor, or your state will be destroyed!

CONCHUBOR — *angry and regal again.* — Are the Sons of Usna buried?

SOLDIER. They are in their grave, but no earth is thrown.

CONCHUBOR. Let me see them. Open the tent! (*Soldier opens back of tent and shows grave.*) Where are my fighters?

SOLDIER. They are gone to Emain.

CONCHUBOR — *to Deirdre.*— There are none to harm you. Stay here until I come again.

> [*Goes out with Soldier. Deirdre looks round for a moment, then goes up slowly and looks into grave. She crouches down and begins swaying herself backwards and forwards, keening softly. At first her words are not heard, then they become clear.*

DEIRDRE. It's you three will not see age or death coming — you that were my company when the fires on the hill-tops were put out and the stars were our friends only. I'll turn my thoughts back from this night, that's pitiful for want of pity, to the time it was your rods and cloaks made a little tent for me where there'd be a birch tree making shelter and a dry stone; though from this day my own fingers will be making a tent for me, spreading out my hairs and they knotted with the rain.

[*Lavarcham and Old Woman come in stealthily on right.*

DEIRDRE — *not seeing them.*— It is I, Deirdre, will be crouching in a dark place; I, Deirdre, that was young with Naisi, and brought sorrow to his grave in Emain.

OLD WOMAN. Is that Deirdre broken down that was so light and airy?

LAVARCHAM. It is, surely, crying out over their grave. [*She goes to Deirdre.*

DEIRDRE. It will be my share from this out to be making lamentation on his stone always, and I crying for a love will be the like of a star shining on a little harbour by the sea.

LAVARCHAM — *coming forward.*— Let you rise up, Deirdre, and come off while there are none to heed us, the way I'll find you shelter and some friend to guard you.

DEIRDRE. To what place would I go away from Naisi? What are the woods without Naisi or the sea shore?

LAVARCHAM — *very coaxingly.* — If it is that way you'd be, come till I find you a sunny place where you'll be a great wonder they'll call the queen of sorrows; and you'll begin taking a pride to be sitting up pausing and dreaming when the summer comes.

DEIRDRE.   It was the voice of Naisi that was strong in summer — the voice of Naisi that was sweeter than pipes playing, but from this day will be dumb always.

LAVARCHAM — *to Old Woman.* — She doesn't heed us at all. We'll be hard set to rouse her.

OLD WOMAN. If we don't the High King will rouse her, coming down beside her with the rage of battle in his blood, for how could Fergus stand against him?

LAVARCHAM — *touching Deirdre with her hand.* — There's a score of woman's years in store for you, and you'd best choose will you start living them beside the man you hate, or being your own mistress in the west or south?

DEIRDRE.   It is not I will go on living after Ainnle and after Ardan. After Naisi I will not have a lifetime in the world.

OLD WOMAN — *with excitement.* — Look, Lavarcham! There's a light leaving the Red

Branch.   Conchubor and his lot will be coming quickly with a torch of bog-deal for her marriage, throwing a light on her three comrades.

DEIRDRE — *startled*—Let us throw down clay on my three comrades. Let us cover up Naisi along with Ainnle and Ardan, they that were the pride of Emain. (*Throwing in clay*.) There is Naisi was the best of three, the choicest of the choice of many. It was a clean death was your share, Naisi; and it is not I will quit your head, when it's many a dark night among the snipe and plover that you and I were whispering together. It is not I will quit your head, Naisi, when it's many a night we saw the stars among the clear trees of Glen da Ruadh, or the moon pausing to rest her on the edges of the hills.

OLD WOMAN. Conchubor is coming, surely. I see the glare of flames throwing a light upon his cloak.

LAVARCHAM — *e a g e r l y.*— Rise up, Deirdre, and come to Fergus, or be the High King's slave for ever!

DEIRDRE — *imperiously.*— I will not leave Naisi, who has left the whole world scorched and desolate. I will not go away when there is no light in the heavens, and no

flower in the earth under them, but is saying
to me that it is Naisi who is gone for ever.

CONCHUBOR — *behind.*— She is here.
Stay a little back. (*Lavarcham and Old
Woman go into the shadow on left as Conchubor comes in. With excitement, to
Deirdre.*) Come forward and leave Naisi the
way I've left charred timber and a smell of
burning in Emain Macha, and a heap of rub-
bish in the storehouse of many crowns.

DEIRDRE — *more awake to what is round
her.*— What are crowns and Emain Macha,
when the head that gave them glory is this
place, Conchubor, and it stretched upon the
gravel will be my bed to-night?

CONCHUBOR.   Make an end of talk of
Naisi, for I've come to bring you to Dundealgan since Emain is destroyed.

[*Conchubor makes a movement towards
her.*

DEIRDRE — *with a tone that stops him.*—
Draw a little back from Naisi, who is young
for ever. Draw a little back from the white
bodies I am putting under a mound of clay
and grasses that are withered — a mound will
have a nook for my own self when the end is
come.

CONCHUBOR — *roughly.*— Let you rise

up and come along with me in place of growing crazy with your wailings here.

DEIRDRE.   It's yourself has made a crazy story, and let you go back to your arms, Conchubor, and to councils where your name is great, for in this place you are an old man and a fool only.

CONCHUBOR.   If I've folly, I've sense left not to lose the thing I've bought with sorrow and the deaths of many. .

[*He moves towards her.*

DEIRDRE.   Do not raise a hand to touch me.

CONCHUBOR.   There are other hands to touch you.   My fighters are set round in among the trees.

DEIRDRE.   Who'll fight the grave, Conchubor, and it opened on a dark night?

LAVARCHAM — *eagerly.* — There   are steps in the wood.   I hear the call of Fergus and his men.

CONCHUBOR — *furiously.*— Fergus cannot stop me.   I am more powerful than he is, though I am defeated and old.

FERGUS — *comes in to Deirdre; a red glow is seen behing the grove.*— I have destroyed Emain, and now I'll guard you all

times, Deirdre, though it was I, without
knowledge, brought Naisi to his grave.

CONCHUBOR. It's not you will guard
her, for my whole armies are gathering. Rise
up, Deirdre, for you are mine surely.

FERGUS — *coming between them.*— I am
come between you.

CONCHUBOR — *w i l d l y.*— When I've
killed Naisi and his brothers, is there any man
that I will spare? And is it you will stand
against me, Fergus, when it's seven years
you've seen me getting my death with rage
in Emain?

FERGUS. It's I, surely, will stand against
a thief and a traitor.

DEIRDRE — *stands up and sees the light
from Emain.*— Draw a little back with the
squabbling of fools when I am broken up
with misery. (*She turns round.*) I see the
flames of Emain starting upward in the dark
night; and because of me there will be weasels
and wild cats crying on a lonely wall where
there were queens and armies and red gold,
the way there will be a story told of a ruined
city and a raving king and a woman will be
young for ever. (*She looks round.*) I see
the trees naked and bare, and the moon
shining. Little moon, little moon of Alban,

it's lonesome you'll be this night, and to-morrow night, and long nights after, and you pacing the woods beyond Glen Laoi, looking every place for Deirdre and Naisi, the two lovers who slept so sweetly with each other.

FERGUS — *going to Conchubor's right and whispering.* — Keep back, or you will have the shame of pushing a bolt on a queen who is out of her wits.

CONCHUBOR. It is I who am out of my wits, with Emain in flames, and Deirdre raving, and my own heart gone within me.

DEIRDRE — *in a high and quiet tone.* — I have put away sorrow like a shoe that is worn out and muddy, for it is I have had a life that will be envied by great companies. It was not by a low birth I made kings uneasy, and they sitting in the halls of Emain. It was not a low thing to be chosen by Conchubor, who was wise, and Naisi had no match for bravery. It is not a small thing to be rid of grey hairs, and the loosening of the teeth. (*With a sort of triumph.*) It was the choice of lives we had in the clear woods, and in the grave, we're safe, surely. . . .

CONCHUBOR. She will do herself harm.

DEIRDRE — *showing Naisi's knife.* — I have a little key to unlock the prison of Naisi

you'd shut upon his youth for ever. Keep
back, Conchubor; for the High King who is
your master has put his hands between us.
(*She half turns to the grave.*) It was sorrows
were foretold, but great joys were my share
always; yet it is a cold place I must go to be
with you, Naisi; and it's cold your arms will
be this night that were warm about my neck
so often. . . . It's a pitiful thing to be talking out when your ears are shut to me. It's
a pitiful thing, Conchubor, you have done this
night in Emain; yet a thing will be a joy and
triumph to the ends of life and time.

> [*She presses knife into her heart and
> sinks into the grave. Conchubor and
> Fergus go forward. The red glow
> fades, leaving stage very dark.*

FERGUS. Four white bodies are laid
down together; four clear lights are quenched
in Ireland. (*He throws his sword into the
grave.*) There is my sword that could not
shield you — my four friends that were the
dearest always. The flames of Emain have
gone out: Deirdre is dead and there is none to
keen her. That is the fate of Deirdre and
the children of Usna, and for this night, Conchubor, our war is ended.   [*He goes out.*

LAVARCHAM. I have a little hut where you can rest, Conchubor; there is a great dew falling.

CONCHUBOR — *with the voice of an old man.*— Take me with you. I'm hard set to see the way before me.

OLD WOMAN. This way, Conchubor.

[*They go out.*

LAVARCHAM — *beside the grave.*— Deirdre is dead, and Naisi is dead; and if the oaks and stars could die for sorrow, it's a dark sky and a hard and naked earth we'd have this night in Emain.

CURTAIN

APPENDIX

DEIRDRE OF THE SORROWS was first produced at the Abbey Theatre, Dublin, on Thursday, January 13th, 1910, with the following cast:

Lavarcham	SARA ALLGOOD
Old Woman	EILEEN O'DOHERTY
Owen	J. A. O'ROURKE
Conchubor	ARTHUR SINCLAIR
Fergus	SYDNEY J. MORGAN
Deirdre	MAIRE O'NEILL
Naisi	FRED O'DONOVAN
Ainnle	J. M. KERRIGAN
Ardan	JOHN CARRICK
Two Soldiers	{ AMBROSE POWER HARRY YOUNG

THE ANDOVER PRESS
U. S. A.